Book design

John Trevitt

Cambridge University Press

Cambridge

London   New York   New Rochelle

Melbourne   Sydney

Published by the Press Syndicate of the University of Cambridge
The Pitt Building, Trumpington Street, Cambridge CB2 1RP
32 East 57th Street, New York, NY 10022, USA
296 Beaconsfield Parade, Middle Park, Melbourne 3206,
  Australia

© Cambridge University Press 1980

First published 1980

Printed in Great Britain at the University Press, Cambridge

Library of Congress cataloguing in publication data
Trevitt, John, 1932–
Book design.
(Cambridge authors' and publishers' guides)
Includes bibliographies and indexes.
1. Book design.   I. Title.   II. Series.
Z116.A3T72   070.5'3   79–20194
ISBN 0 521 29741 9

Contents

It has been said that 'the printing of books should be invisible'. The text is the author's and the act of setting it in type gives it a formal standing and authority which cannot be claimed for mere typescript. It is the purpose of typographical design to lay this text before the reader in a style which is at once clear, approachable, unobtrusive and handsome. The designer attempts to articulate the various elements of the text; to relate to it illustrations which may be necessary or useful to an understanding of the verbal text, or simply decorative; and to harmonise these elements within the context of the chosen format, materials and modes of production. As soon as commercial considerations obtain – as soon, in other words, as people feel anxious about the price of the book, which is not uncommon in virtually all areas of book publishing – the pursuit of these ideals is complicated by the need to save money. This can be done in various ways, some more tactful than others, and it is an important part of the designer's job to design for economy with no loss of clarity and the least possible loss of quality.

The designer should be involved with a book throughout its preparatory stages and continuously thereafter until he can pass an early finished copy. He should get the approval of the editor (and, when appropriate, the author and the sales departments) for his choice of format and materials and his layout of text, illustrations and jacket; and he should provide specifications for setting, printing and binding. The printer may be asked to estimate costs on the basis of these specifications; the copy-editor will have them before him as he works on the text; and the printer will follow them in setting the text. The designer should have at least a hand in the commissioning of illustrations, pass all stages of corrected proofs, oversee the preparation of any paste-up, and approve printed sheets and an early copy of the book.

We shall see that the decisions which determine the form of the finished book are closely interrelated and cannot by any means always be taken in the same sequence. Probably the choice of printing process is the most likely to have a significant bearing on the total production cost and is therefore the most likely to be made first.

The choice is almost exclusively between the offset litho process, printing from planographic plates prepared photographically from an image on film; or letterpress printing, either flatbed from type and blocks, or on rotary presses from relief plates (made either by moulding type or by photo-etching from an image on film). The unique characteristic of printing from type is its crisp impression into the paper, and this of course cannot be counterfeited by the litho process. On the other hand, letterpress printing is accompanied by some slight thickening of the image, and litho at its best produces a finer and more precise result. In general terms, letterpress is losing ground, offset litho is gaining; but letterpress is far from dead, and may be appropriate if the run is short and the text complex and lightly, if at all, illustrated, or if there is an overriding wish for the characteristic impression of letterpress. For runs below two thousand a book may best be printed from type (Monotype single characters, or Linotype or Intertype lines, called 'slugs'). For such short runs letterpress printing costs much the same as litho, and Monotype setting in particular is suitable for the complex make-up and repeated correction typical of academic monographs. There are, however, arguments in favour of litho printing even for some kinds of short-run work: if the book is likely to be reprinted it is useful to have standing film from the first impression; illustrations cost very little to print compared with the cost of making blocks for letterpress; halftones may be printed in the text on virtually any paper, whereas letterpress halftones demand art paper and may have to be printed separately from the text; it may be advantageous to compose the text on an IBM Composer or a filmsetter, which normally leads to litho printing; an unexceptional book with an undemanding text may lend itself to run-of-the-mill treatment on a litho mini-web press, on which surprisingly short runs are economical.

For runs of two thousand or more, the only class of book for which letterpress can compete on price is the pocket paperback, printed flexographically on reel-fed rotary presses from rubber or plastic plates. For all other work letterpress is a luxury, afforded for its characteristics, and offset litho is the norm, though photogravure (printing long runs from photographically prepared intaglio plates) and collotype (printing very short runs from a screenless plate which closely counterfeits continuous tone) may be appropriate for occasional jobs suited to their characteristic images and price scales.

The choice of paper for letterpress printing is often critical, and has to take account of the typeface used, line blocks (if any) in the text, and the desired bulk of the book in relation to its extent. Some kind of fairly soft antique wove is usual, but a harder-surfaced machine finished (MF) is more appropriate to fine line blocks and to certain typefaces. A clay-coated, shiny and relatively expensive art paper is essential for all but the coarsest-screened halftone blocks. Litho is less fussy and can print any image on almost any surface, though fine-screen halftones will benefit from a smooth surface and all halftones are sharpest on art paper.

Next must come the choice of format (page size), since so many details of design and layout follow from it. The page size depends in its turn on the intended use of the book, on the textual and illustrative content, on the extent, on the way it is to be printed and bound, and on the paper to be used. The range of reel and sheet sizes in which paper is stocked (by mills, merchants and printers) is severely limited, and, because paper is seldom made to special order in small quantities, for short-run books it is most economical to base the format of the book on one of these standard sizes, folding the sheet (usually in half) repeatedly until the appropriate size is reached. A quad demy sheet, for example, carries 16 pages of metric demy 4to, 32 pages of metric demy 8vo, 'to view' (on each side of the sheet). The standard sheet sizes and the standard page sizes derived from them are given in millimetres on p. 4. It should perhaps be said that printing presses, both letterpress and litho, come in a wide variety of sizes, few exactly matching the standard metric sheet sizes of paper.

Metric Crown	768 × 1008	4to, 246 × 189; 8vo, 186 × 123
Metric Tall		
Crown	816 × 1056	8vo, 198 × 129
Metric Demy	888 × 1128	4to, 276 × 219; 8vo, 216 × 138
Metric Royal	960 × 1272	4to, 312 × 237; 8vo, 234 × 156
RAO	860 × 1220	A4, 297 × 210; A5, 210 × 148

There are two important categories of book whose format is based on the size of the printing press, rather than on the available sheet sizes. The first and more obvious is the book printed 'on the web', i.e. from reels not sheets of paper. Web-fed presses vary considerably in size, but it is always most economical to print on paper as wide as the press can accommodate, which determines the depth of the page; and all of them have only a limited number of 'cut-offs', which determine the width of the page. (These considerations are made doubly important by the fact that in long-run work, which is usually printed on the web for economy, the main costs are those of paper and printing, whereas composition and origination are the prime costs of short-run work.) Similarly, it is usual when planning the production of long-run sheet-fed work – particularly if the extent has to be kept down and the page has therefore to carry as many words as possible, as in some school-books – to base the format on the largest sheet that the selected press can print, since the quantity of paper required should be enough to justify a special making. (A trap here awaits whoever has to order a small reprint, which the wise designer will point out in good time.)

So much for the principles behind the choice of format. The practical decisions have many factors to take into account. Use should be the first: is the book to be carried in a pocket or a satchel? read in bed, in an armchair, at a table or desk? used in the kitchen, the garage, the countryside? read through (and then perhaps discarded), studied, looked at, or used only for reference? Then, of course, content: illustrations may require, or at least be improved by, a large page; the extent of an extremely long book can be kept to a minimum by simply packing as many words as possible on as large a page as possible; a wide measure will minimise the number of mathematical equations and chemical formulae which are too long to fit the line and have to be broken; a dictionary or other work intended for occasional reference may be set in small type to a narrow measure in two (or more) columns; verse sits well on a narrow page. Marketing considerations may well suggest that an important book be made to look 'important' by its large format.

Filmsetting is advancing hand in hand with litho printing, naturally enough since the filmset image can most easily be exposed on a litho plate (though nylon relief plates for rotary letterpress and the Cameron belt press are also made from a film image). However, many typesetters prefer to produce the filmset image on bromide paper, and this has then to be photographed – as does 'cold' composition from IBM Composers, word-processors and typewriters – giving the same options. The obvious thing to do with metal type, once set, is to print from it, but there are other options: it may be moulded for the production of rotary relief plates, or reproduction proofs ('repro pulls') may be taken for photographing. Filmsetting is, as we shall see, all too often hampered by poor typography, but is helped by being closely allied with computer-assisted setting. This offers advantages in a number of areas: faster setting; text storage in both plain ('idiot') and typographically-encoded states, permitting different format designs from one keyboarding, and easy updating; automated page make-up; and text manipulation on a screen. A job which requires a large number of founts, or sizes, or faces, or special characters, will best be set on a filmsetter, which should have them readily available. (Of the alternatives, IBM Composer is least suitable because of the frequent changes of 'golfball' that would be necessitated; slug-setting is usually inappropriate because most printers use it for setting straightforward work and are not equipped to deal with complexities; and Monotype is probably the best because of the inherent flexibility of its single-character system and the extended matrix cases available for some typefaces.) There are, however, very many different kinds of filmsetter, and the designer will find it essential to know well the capacities and disadvantages of all the machines he is called upon to design for.

These considerations – format, paper, mode of typesetting, method of printing – are of course interdependent, and they cannot be arranged in any invariable causal sequence. Most decisions probably stem from the choice of printing process, which is almost always dictated by considerations of economy, but if the text can be set properly only in hot metal, or if the format is predetermined by some consideration other than the cost of printing, choice of printing process comes second.

Because nearly all the typefaces used for bookwork are modern adaptations of some of the best historical models, they tend in their hot-metal versions to be most sympathetic to the sort of paper which was in particular favour when their models were first cut. This usually means in practice that types dating back before the nineteenth century look best, when printed letterpress, on rather soft, off-white antique wove and that more modern faces prefer a harder, smoother MF. This is only a generalisation and there are a number of exceptions to it. (When hot-metal type is converted by way of repro pulls for litho printing, or when it is printed on art paper, then it is only the more robust faces that can safely be used without the risk of a thin, starved result.) There is a hard core of hot-metal faces that are well suited to letterpress bookwork and quite widely available: Bembo, Garamond, Plantin, Ehrhardt, Baskerville, Imprint, Times; with perhaps as many again that are less commonly available or particularly suited to unusual work of one kind or another: Granjon, Fournier, Scotch Roman, Modern, Juliana, Spectrum. The above (many of which are available for slugsetting by Linotype or Intertype as well as single-character Monotype setting) with the occasional use of such decorative, not to say idiosyncratic, faces as Centaur, Poliphilus, Bell or Perpetua, formed the more-than-adequate repertoire of book designers until the advent of film.

Fast, clean setting into film seemed to offer the promised land to printers and production managers already aware of the economies to be derived from litho printing; yet hot metal and, to a lesser extent, letterpress have survived and competed successfully, to the time of writing. This is due to caution and lack of capital in printing, to publishing conservatism and a sharper awareness of the folly of overprinting, and in no small measure to the ineptitude, early and in many cases continuing, of numerous adaptations of the traditional faces for filmsetting. A prime characteristic of letterpress printing, the impression of type into the paper, is accompanied by the phenomenon called squash: a slight thickening of the image due to the pressure on the ink at the moment of transfer to the page. The design and printing of hot-metal faces clearly cannot be discussed without reference to this effect, yet it seems to have been commonly ignored in transfer to film. Again, letter designs in the various sizes of hot-metal typefaces are by no means identical, the smaller sizes tending to be somewhat rounder and with comparatively large counters (spaces within letter-forms), but these careful distinctions have rarely survived the transfer to

film. The choice of typeface for filmsetting is made difficult: by these considerations which effectively rule out the film equivalents of some favourite hot-metal faces; by the low quality of the output of certain photosetters, resulting in poor alignment and poor letter-fit (the relation of one letter to its neighbours and to the spaces in between); and, it has to be said, by the vast and ever-changing range of photosetting equipment around and the scarcity of accurate information about it. At the time of writing, the safest recommendations, typographically speaking, are the various Monophoto and Linofilm/Linotron machines and the VIP. Filmset typefaces differ, not only from their hot-metal models, but also from one make of photosetter to another, and it is quite impossible to specify with any confidence unless one can see a representative sample of the typefaces in question, in the appropriate sizes, set on the kind of photosetter that is to set the job. Certain traditional faces usually look well when filmset: Garamond, Plantin, Ehrhardt, Baskerville, Times. New typefaces especially designed for filmsetting have appeared, though few of them are truly new in the sense of having no apparent historical model, few are widely available, and few have won themselves a place in the designer's everyday repertoire. Of the new arrivals, Sabon, Lectura and Palatino are probably the most useful.

The designer's choice of typeface is of course usually restricted to those available at the production department's chosen typesetter, and – if the text contains complexities – to those equipped with the necessary special characters. Mathematics, for example, requires symbols and special 'sorts' usually available only in Times or Modern No. 7. Transliterated Arabic, phonetics, linguistics and chemistry all require special characters. Words in 'exotic' 'alphabets' such as Arabic, Hebrew or Chinese are almost invariably set separately from the surrounding English text and dropped in later, but Greek and Russian can be composed and cast with English using an extended Monotype matrix-case, on the IBM Composer, and on a good filmsetter. Choice is further restricted, particularly in relation to letterpress printing, to those faces suitable for the paper to be used. The older, more delicate faces do not, on the whole, look well on any coated stock; they look all wrong on art paper and prefer the softer antique wove to an MF. On the other hand it is difficult to realise the merits of the most popular face of all, Times New Roman (to give it its proper name for once), except on a smooth finish.

Yet another major factor in the choice of typeface is the necessity of fitting commercially-published books into marketable extents – particularly paperbacks and other long-run books, which must also make even workings without oddments. The reading public seems to be wary of very long books and is said to be positively antipathetic to short ones, and a lot can be done typographically to fit long and short books into moderate extents. This is achieved partly by attention to narrowness (and roundness) in letter forms; but it is based more firmly on the proportions of x-height to type size. This is the explanation of

the phenomenon of 'appearing size', whereby 13 pt Perpetua, 12 pt Bembo, 11 pt Garamond and 10 pt

An ascending and
a descending
letter, showing
some of the parts
and dimensions of
the face

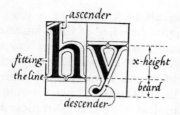

Some of the parts
of the letter

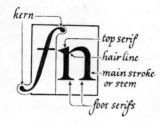

Some of the more
important parts of
a type

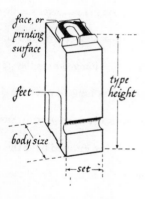

The three most
common kinds of
serif

From Hugh Williamson, *Methods of Book Design*, second edition,
Oxford University Press, 1966. Reproduced by permission of the
author and publisher.

Times all look much of a size. It is in fact their x-heights (the size of their lower-case letters without ascenders or descenders, such as a, c, e, x) which are similar, while Perpetua, at one extreme, has very long extenders and Times very short ones. So, when space has to be saved, Times set solid will be the most economical of these examples, Perpetua the least, since the page might accommodate 45 lines of 10 pt but only 36 lines of 13 pt. Conversely, if a long short story has to look like a novel, it may be 'driven out' by being set in Perpetua and leaded (with extra space between the lines). Although Perpetua is a somewhat mannered face, the latter will be easy to

Below: Some popular hot-metal typefaces shown in 10 pt

Baskerville	The quick brown fox jumped over the slow lazy dog.
Bell	The quick brown fox jumped over the slow lazy dog.
Bembo	The quick brown fox jumped over the slow lazy dog.
Ehrhardt	The quick brown fox jumped over the slow lazy dog.
Fournier	The quick brown fox jumped over the slow lazy dog.
Garamond	The quick brown fox jumped over the slow lazy dog.
Granjon	The quick brown fox jumped over the slow lazy dog.
Imprint	The quick brown fox jumped over the slow lazy dog.
Juliana	The quick brown fox jumped over the slow lazy dog.
Modern	The quick brown fox jumped over the slow lazy dog.
Perpetua	The quick brown fox jumped over the slow lazy dog.
Plantin	The quick brown fox jumped over the slow lazy dog.
Poliphilus	The quick brown fox jumped over the slow lazy dog.
Scotch Roman	The quick brown fox jumped over the slow lazy dog.
Spectrum	The quick brown fox jumped over the slow lazy dog.
Times	The quick brown fox jumped over the slow lazy dog.

read; the Times page will be tough going because it breaks one of the basic rules of book typography, which states that the space between the words should be less than the space between the lines. Obedience to this rule is the main guide which takes the eye from the end of one line to the beginning of the next without risk of confusion or 'doubling'. Faces with long extenders, such as Perpetua and Bembo, can safely be set solid without risk of violating this rule, but a face with a large x-height in relation to the length of its extenders benefits greatly from leading.

There is only one other rule of any consequence, though it too is frequently broken, usually because a long book has to be squeezed into an extent which can be manufactured and sold at an acceptable price. In normal reading, the reader's eye should be focussed on the middle of the line and apprehend, or guess, the words at the periphery. If the line is too long, or contains too many words, this process is slowed up, and the reader fatigued, by the need to read more words, perhaps to read them all, and to travel consciously from one line to the next. If the line contains too few words, the number of lines is undesirably increased, and either the variable spaces between the words vary too much from line to line, or, if the setting is unjustified, the line-endings look too ragged – more of this later. The ideal line length depends on the way the book is read: 20–21 picas is ideal for a pocket paperback, 22–26 picas for a cased book held in the hand, 27–32 picas for a larger book read at a desk or table. The ideal number of words per line seems to be 10–12. It should be said that these criteria relate to continuous prose: most books intended for reference can be set more tightly and in smaller type, though this is less true of books for frequent reference such as cookery books and other instruction manuals than it is of dictionaries. Really small type set in narrow columns with little or no leading squeezes the largest possible number of words on the page, but cannot be read for long without severe discomfort.

The choice of page size, type size and measure leads of course to fixing the margins, though they will already be implicit, if ill-defined, in the designer's mind. All these elements depend on each other if the page is to look attractive and to be appropriate to the book's purpose, the hallmark of good plain book design. But it is a pair of facing pages that the reader sees on opening the book, and in fixing margins the designer knows that they must be designed as a unity. There are two useful formulae for the proportions of space allocated to the four margins of the traditional page, ratios read clockwise from the back on a recto page as either $1\frac{1}{2}:2:3:4$ or $2:3:4:5$. Both ensure that the sum of the back margins is equal to the foredge margin, which anchors the type areas firmly on the width of the open book. Both place the type area well above the mathematical centre, in obedience to the phenomenon of optical centre, and both ensure adequate space in the foot margin for the reader's thumbs as he holds the book open. Both need to be tested by eye, the best judge for every book, but either should yield a comfortably conventional arrangement of the type on the page if the type area is between one-half and two-thirds of the page area and if the typographical layout is itself conventional. Books with unusually small type areas, or a totally unconventional typographical layout, can be designed only by eye. Books with large type areas, large that is in relation to the page size, such as pocket paperbacks, cannot afford any luxury in their margins, and must rely on such a ratio as $2:2\frac{1}{2}:3:3\frac{1}{2}$, really no more than is needed to ensure that the type will not bleed if the book is carelessly trimmed. To the 'visible' back margins must then be added an allowance of about 3 mm for the trim in the case of most adhesive-bound books, or for the edge of the page which disappears into the back in the case of a rounded-and-backed sewn book (a little less for flat- or square-backed cased books), and it has to be remembered that this 3 mm is part of the trimmed page width of the sewn book.

Having established measure, margins, text typeface, size and interlinear space (leading), the designer will want to develop the idea of text layout which lay

behind these choices: the detailing of headings,
subheadings, quotations, tables and footnotes, and
the handling of illustrations. The first question is,
however, is the page to be centred or asymmetrical?,
and the answer should be followed through the
articulation of all parts of the book.

One decision which may precede this essential
question establishes whether or not the text is to be
justified; in other words, whether the word spacing
is to be fixed, as in verse setting, with a ragged right-
hand edge, or variable, so that all lines are driven
out to fill the measure ('justified'). Typewriters and
some IBM Composers cannot justify: all other typesetting equipment can, and does at no extra cost, so
that this can be treated as an aesthetic decision
(though printers usually justify unless told not to).
There are at least three ways of not justifying, and
the prudent designer will specify beforehand which
is wanted: (1) 'Break no words', which makes for
very ragged setting but may be useful for children's
books and foreign-language texts; (2) 'Break words as
if justifying', which is nearest to conventional setting;
or (3) 'Break words to keep short lines to at least
x picas' (x being normally 2 picas less than the
measure), which probably makes for the least ragged
right-hand edge. Proponents of justified setting argue
that variable word spacing is less distracting than a
ragged right-hand edge (and that the convention of
justifying is so established that it cannot be flouted).
Proponents of unjustified setting argue the opposite
(and, in the case of (1) above, that for certain texts
the elimination of word breaks is of benefit to the
reader). Both say 'particularly in narrow-measure
work'. Unjustified setting is no longer either trendy
or dangerous, and designers can be left to choose the
appropriate style for each book. It is worth bearing
in mind that unjustified setting can be used for
inherently ragged copy, for example lists, short notes
and indexes, in an otherwise justified text; and that
because it can be set to a slightly wider measure than
justified text without appearing to fill more of the
page, it is useful as an aid to 'packing in' a long book.

It is impossible to blend any kind of centred layout
satisfactorily with unjustified setting, because so few

text lines, on some pages none at all, fill the measure
on which headings and folios would be automatically
centred; but the reverse does not obtain, and justified
text can be accommodated in centred and asymmetrical designs. Once the early printers had learnt
the knack of justifying each line by varying the word
spacing within it, justified setting and centred typography were seldom challenged as the unquestionable
norm until recently. That they remain, for most
kinds of book, the traditional elements of book design
is due to conservatism; to the fact that centring is
safer than asymmetry; and, paradoxically, to the
ability of modern typesetting equipment to centre

and justify automatically. Centring is safe because
there are no forces within the layout of each page to
disturb the balance of the two-page opening, itself a
restful unit with optically centred type areas and
optically balanced vertical margins; and because
centring, like other elements of typographical design,
obeys convention. It is safe too in the sense that a
slight miscalculation, or a last-minute need to over-
trim through undersize paper having been supplied,
will result only in a dull book. An asymmetrical
design, on the other hand, depends for its success on
balancing the dynamic conflict between the various
uncentred elements: it is not as easy to get this right,
and it can all too easily be ruined. Art Nouveau, the
private press movement, the Bauhaus, and the post-
war generations of book designers have all chipped
away at the fortress of convention, and asymmetry is
now acceptable – in some areas, indeed, it is respec-
table, even predictable.

Certain kinds of copy lend themselves to a centred
layout. A prose work which contains verse quotations,
for example, normally looks rather unconvincing if
the quotations are not visually centred on the prose
measure. Small decorative illustrations look best
when centred. Any typographical design which aims
to copy or allude to pre-Morris typography must
certainly be centred. Beyond this is the matter of
formality: because the centred style carries the mass
of tradition, it is to be preferred for a definitive, or
would-be definitive, text.

Asymmetrical design is used widely – perhaps

through association with unjustified setting, and because it is not (yet) traditional – for informal texts such as novels and booklets. It has practical advantages: for mathematical and scientific books (in which frequent broken-off equations may be ranged tidily on a fixed indent rather than centred); for books of letters or similar documents which are themselves asymmetrical; and for catalogues or other books containing lists, best arranged on a left-hand axis. It is preferable for unjustified work such as books of verse and those set on the typewriter or IBM Composer.

In many books the most obvious feature of the design is the system of headings, subheadings and pageheads. Occasionally, the decision, centred or asymmetrical, may rest on these: centred they are formal, prominent, even dominant, whereas they become much less insistent when ranged to the left of an asymmetrical page. Again, the various grades of subheading, if articulated through a range of small capitals, bold and italic, will be more consciously displayed if centred; but if they be numbered decimally (and therefore not in need of variegated treatment) they will readily range with their numbers flush to the left-hand margin. The decimal system seems most at home in a scientific text, but offers the only unambiguous system of defining more than three grades of subheading. Three grades ought to be enough for all but the most densely-packed, rigorously organised text anyway, and can be expressed with the conventional small capitals, italics and, perhaps, bold, though sans-serif, Lumitype, Dymo, and IBM faces have no true small capitals and some hot-metal and filmset faces have no related bold. Some bold faces are very heavy indeed, but even the comparatively light semi-bolds such as Ehrhardt and Baskerville can be black enough to spoil the colour of an otherwise carefully balanced page. The temptation to 'liven up' the design of a book by the use of different typefaces in text and subheadings is always present but usually to be resisted, since harmony is hard to come by and contrast may be altogether too lively for the reader's comfort. If, however, the designer is determined to mix his types, he might look at the possibilities of combining sans-serif sub-headings with seriffed text, so long as the text face is not as determinedly antiquarian as, say, Van Dijck or Centaur.

Pageheads, also called running headlines, are subject to the same discipline of page design as are subheadings, though it is possible, because of their fixed position and their function as items of reference rather than as parts of the text, to set them in comparatively small type and to determine by eye their position in relation to the text and the cut edges of the page. Since the whole point of having pageheads is for quick reference, it follows that their function is obstructed if they are more than five or six words long; wordy book, part or chapter titles, or subheadings, should wherever possible be so reduced for use in pageheads.

In a book that has no part or chapter titles or subheadings, such as is the case with many novels, the pagehead has no useful function to serve and may be omitted. It may be retained to help push out the extent of a short book, or because of its decorative quality, in which case there is no option but to repeat the title of the book at the head of every page.

The book's structure of major headings (running through the half-title, title page, preliminary pages, part and chapter titles, and end-pages) should be so designed as to reflect or harmonise with the typography of the text, subheadings and pageheads. It is possible, as with subheadings, to achieve a pleasing contrast using a different typeface from that used in the text, and as the major headings stand apart from the text by virtue of their size and the space beneath them it is easier to mix types here than in the sub-headings. The designer might try a combination of a seriffed text with a strong, lively, seriffed display face (such as Goudy Bold or Garamond bold italic – frailer or more idiosyncratic faces will fail to hold the proper balance). Even here, however, it is safer to use the text face. Whatever face is chosen for the major headings, at least as important will be the choice of type size, alphabet and position on the page, all of course interdependent. The size that might seem about right for the staccato phrases used to head the chapters of an adventure novel would probably look out of place in a learned monograph (and in the latter case would probably result in a six-line chapter heading). The capitals that could be used to give formality to the latter might look simply dull in the former context. The use of modest sizes of upper and lower case for non-fiction headings, once frowned on as insufficiently formal, now seems perfectly acceptable, particularly, perhaps, in asymmetrical layouts, where the irregularity inherent in upper and lower case composition does not upset the delicate balance of the page. A pleasing effect, and a particularly coherent piece of book design, may be achieved by using the same convention, italic upper and lower case, perhaps, in various sizes for sub-headings, pageheads and major headings.

Certain typefaces and typographical arrangements lend themselves to ornamentation appropriate to the text. Printers' flowers, for example, look well in a work of history or literature; but they depend for success on a centred layout and on deriving from the same period of typographical history as the typeface they embellish. They ought, too, to complement, or at least not to contradict, the historical context of the book itself: Renaissance flowers would not suit books on Queen Victoria or Nazi Germany. Rules often earn their keep: short measures of thick-and-thin with typefaces that have some vertical stress, such as Bodoni and Scotch Roman; a fine rule below page-heads set in small capitals; or a text-measure $1\frac{1}{2}$ pt rule used to set off an asymmetrical chapter heading. It is, however, all too easy to play safe when doubtful of a design, by including rules whose function is akin to that of the pit-prop.

The chapter number may be run in with the title, or it can look well placed higher on the page. Here the word 'chapter' can be retained, and set quite small with the number; or the number itself can be picked out and either set in some decorative face or ornamented. This is particularly attractive in a centred design, if for some reason the major headings have to be in a small size of capitals. In the same way, part titles can either be set in the style of the chapter headings, or turned into a decorative feature of the book – particularly if they fall alone on recto pages. Part headings that are placed immediately above chapter headings, and chapter headings that run on rather than starting new pages, inevitably have to be treated more discreetly, since their effect has to be achieved in comparatively limited space.

The headings of preliminary pages, such as the lists of contents and illustrations, acknowledgements, preface and introduction, and of end-pages, including appendices, bibliography, notes and index, are commonly set in the style of the chapter headings; but if the latter, happening to be brief, have been set unusually large, it may be better to set the preliminary and end-page headings somewhat smaller, while retaining the same style and ornament (if any). This will avoid any risk that the preliminary pages, in particular, might look overblown.

Another typographical feature prominent in many academic books is the table. The design of tables has been rationalised, and visually very much improved, by the virtual exclusion of vertical rules (which became prohibitively expensive in hot-metal setting) and increasing sophistication in the disposition of space, both vertical and horizontal, between rules set to text measure at head and tail: the heading can be placed above the first rule and any notes below the second. Narrow tables can be centred, or indented, say 3 picas from the left. Wide tables can (particularly if filmset) extend into the margins, or be turned on the page ('landscaped'), or be spread across two facing pages. Sometimes they can be changed into upright tables, by the transposition of their axes. Tables are best set small, say 8 pt or 9 pt, with just enough leading to carry the eye right across the tabular material (in which exercise the eye may be helped across particularly wide tables if the 'stubs', or left-side headings, be numbered with the numbers repeated at the right). The vertical alignment of tabular material and column headings needs particular care, to ensure that it is set out clearly, and also to match the style of the book. Columns of figures are at their clearest with figures in the units column ranged vertically. Non-numerical copy is best judged *ad hoc* and may be ranged at left or right or centred. This is true of column headings also, but here the chosen style must not clash with the text: column headings flush left or right can seriously upset the layout of a centred book. Tabular copy, which is often badly presented, repays careful analysis by the designer and editor: they may find ways of simplifying it or making it clearer, or easier to set. It is occasionally beneficial to transpose the horizontal and vertical headings.

Most quotations from other works are easily enough designed. The first decision to be made is, simply, whether there is any need to distinguish prose quotations typographically from the surrounding text. As often as not there is none, and they can just be enclosed in quotation marks and run into the author's text. If they have to be set off, the question is type size: the same size as the text, or smaller? In a book which also contains footnotes this decision may be complicated, either by a limitation in the sizes of type available, or by too close a similarity between, say 10 pt and 9 pt, or 9 pt and 8 pt. Generally speaking, verse quotations and those prose quotations that make a minimum of five lines look best in small type: prose may be set to the text measure (which contributes to the strength of the page structure); they will attract a few extra points' space above and below (needed to fill the depth of the page); and quotation marks are redundant. Also, in a long book, a few pages may be saved this way. When prose quotations are set in text type they are best indented: left and right if the balance of a centred book is not to be spoilt. The typesetter may then be instructed to leave no extra space above and below, or a half-line. In the latter case, however, quotations which start on one page and finish on the next may end up preceded and followed by a whole line of space, which looks dreadful. (Other dreadful effects, easily avoided, are those achieved by setting quotations in unleaded text type – too black – or small type set on the same body size or line feed as the text – too pale.)

Verse quotations pose a special problem in asymmetrical book design, since they cry out to be centred by eye on the text measure. It is possible to indent them, say 3 picas from the left, but their unsettling effect on the balance of the two-page spread can be decisive. As most verse is readily distinguished from prose, verse quotations can reasonably be set in text type, centred or indented, with no need of extra space above or below (unless there is space between stanzas within a quotation, when the same space should precede and follow it). Verse is always set unjustified, with a fixed word space – slightly wider perhaps than that used in unjustified settings of prose and lists, to assist the reader to read aloud. Care should be taken to select a combination of type size and measure which will accommodate the longest lines of verse, since turnover lines – particularly in verse drama – tend to obscure the structure of the work and to confuse the reader. If the poet chose to start each line with a capital letter, as is generally the case, the designer will probably employ a typeface whose capitals are relatively small and, more important, relatively light – such as Bembo or Fournier rather than, say, Scotch Roman or Imprint.

Many books have notes, generally consisting either of sources and references to works cited, or of substantive but incidental comments. The latter are best set at the foot of the page, but a set of notes consisting largely of references to titles of books and journals is usually best placed at the end of the book. Footnotes are best numbered sequentially from one, starting afresh on each page, or failing that they may be numbered through each chapter. (The latter is the cheaper option in slugsetting, and in those computer-assisted filmsetting systems that are not equipped to provide the former option automatically.) Other devices have been tried, including the 'traditional' recurrent sequence of symbols *, †, ‡, §, ||, ¶; and 1–9, 1–9; 1–19, 1–19; 1–99, 1–99 recurrent numbering sequences. The make-up of pages with long or numerous footnotes is difficult, because of the need to accommodate the text and the notes relating to it on the same page. The type size used should therefore be the smallest that can be easily read. The cleanest footnote layout ranges the note number (which need not be superior, but usually is) flush left, with turn-over lines aligned on the first word. If the notes are long, however, this will cause them to make an extra line or two, and then the arrangement may be reversed, with the number indented and turnovers set to the full measure. Those short notes that make less than half the measure should share a line wherever possible, to save space and to avoid an ugly pool of white space at the foot of the page. The balance of a centred page can be spoilt by any uncentred element (except apparently paragraph ends, which the eye excuses), and in Monotype work, filmsetting and cold composition it is possible to specify that where the notes on a page all fail to fill the measure the longest should be centred and the others aligned on it. (They could all be centred, of course, but that might look precious.)

Endnotes should be numbered through chapters, set unjustified, perhaps, as so many lines are likely not to fill the measure, in type slightly larger than would be used for footnotes, and collected at the back of the book under subheadings giving the number and title of each chapter. If they are all, or nearly all, very short a lot of space can be saved by setting them in two columns. If they are long, with turnovers set to the full measure, the note numbers can usefully be bold. Numbering endnotes by page entails adding the page numbers to the notes in page proof, which is expensive, time-consuming and a waste of space. There is nothing to be said in favour of placing end-notes (or reference lists) at the ends of chapters, since the reader will find them at the end of the book with greater ease. The only exception to this rule is the symposium, of which offprints (reprints of single chapters) may be required.

Bibliographies and lists of references should be set in the same type size as endnotes (which is likely to be the size chosen for small-type quotations), probably unjustified, with turnovers indented two ems. The old habit of listing names in small capitals was rather prettifying for all but the most elegant of literary monographs; but small capitals for frequent short-form author references can be useful.

Indexes have to be set after the rest of the book, when the text has been paged. Normally, they are set in two columns in, roughly, 8/9 pt type – say footnote size; but they sometimes have to be set a little larger or smaller than the ideal to coax the extent of the whole book into one convenient for even workings. As a large number of lines will fall short of the measure, and there will be a very few word spaces in some other lines, indexes should nearly always be set unjustified, though when there are numerous long strings of numbers justifying would look tidier. The simplest system is to indent turnover lines one em; if there are broken-off sub-entries, to indent these one em and turnovers two ems. A more complicated index will have to be judged *ad hoc*: it may be better to identify sub-entries and sub-sub-entries typographically (with italics, bold or small capitals) and to indent them but run turnovers to the full measure. An index which contains a large number of long entries may look clearer in one column. Indexes, particularly elaborate ones, should be designed as simply as possible, to encourage every reader to use them. A really simple index may be set with a fixed space only, and no comma, separating the page numbers.

With the text and end-pages designed, the designer now turns to the preliminary pages. Preface, fore-word and introduction will probably be set like the text. They may be set a size larger if their author is, in some sense, more important than the author of the book; or a size smaller if they are brief preambles to, say, a standard text or a translation. Acknowledgements will probably follow text style and a mere list of publishers and others who have granted routine permission might well be placed at the back of the book, before the index and, if long, set in small type.

The contents list is often the most difficult page in the whole book to design. It should be clear, inviting, and harmonious in style with the text and headings, and it should if possible be complete on one page. If brief, it may be set larger than the text; if composed of short entries, narrower. In text type, it will gain clarity from extra leading. Subheadings (such as part titles) within the list may be set in the style used for subheadings in the text, or perhaps more decoratively. It is frequently the subheadings from the text, beneath their respective chapter titles, that can drive out a contents list undesirably, and the value of including them in the list is always worth questioning. The contents page itself can be omitted from a book in which the individual chapters have no titles. Other lists in the preliminary pages – illustrations, figures, tables – can take their general style from the contents page, and can if long be set in small type. Some of these are of no great value and could be omitted, such as lists of text figures which have no captions and no significance beyond their textual context, or of text illustrations which are merely decorative.

A touch of elegance may be provided in the design of dedication or epigraph (and, indeed, in the design of other displayed epigraphs on part titles or chapter openings); but a touch is enough and overeagerness shows. Prose can be set in text type and the measure reduced, so long as all the copy fits on to the page.

The verso of the title page will face the dedication or epigraph, if any, or the contents page. It probably cannot be made to look attractive; but the unruly material it may carry (publisher's addresses, publication date, copyright notices, publication history, brief acknowledgements, printer's imprint, ISBN, and the British Library or Library of Congress CIP information) can at least be made seemly by being set in one alphabet of a small size (say 9 pt, leaded) of the text face, centred or flush left according to the style of the book. The measure is best kept narrower than that of the text, and temptations to elegant variation (such as a change of alphabet for the printer's imprint) are best avoided.

Traditionally, the title page was the printer's playground. Now it is the designer's, and he may choose from the whole range of typographical expression, from the severe use of carefully spaced text-size capitals to exuberant and elaborate decoration in type or illustration or (if he is careful) both. If there is a frontispiece – an illustration facing the title page, on text or other paper – it is likely to steal the show and the wise designer will allow his title page to act as a typographical foil to it; type cannot overpower a picture and the struggle is never edifying. The same conflict can sometimes be seen on the title page itself, where an illustration – even the publisher's own device – is not at ease with some typographical ornament or 'decorative' typeface. There is usually a case to be made for a flourish of some sort; never for too big a flourish, or too many of them. Probably the right balance will be found if the title page is neither less decorative, nor very much more so, than the chapter headings or part titles. The layout should accord with that of the text, and there are many elegant ways of designing both asymmetrical and centred title pages. Stanley Morrison said that there is no reason why the largest type should be more than twice as large as the text type; and that the title and author's name should be set in capitals, to accord the proper formality to them on this most formal of pages. These are useful comments and provide a safe formula, though not an invariable rule. Safety will be found also in adherence to a maximum of two alphabets, and this is particularly true if one of the alphabets be taken from another face for (and best restricted to) the title and subtitle. This mixing can be done on the title page if nowhere else; and if the designer has introduced a second face for his part or chapter headings in the text, he should usually display it again on the title page even if he favours a plainer style for other preliminary and end-page headings. Many publishers own a device, sometimes (misleadingly) called a colophon, which they like to display on their title pages. Some devices are of venerable antiquity, some of very fine design, and they may lend the book a touch of class. They tend, however, to be powerful on the title page, and their use normally demands sober typography and not infrequently – particularly in the case of shields – a centred layout. It is, besides, rather difficult to arrange a convincing and uncluttered display incorporating both a frontispiece and a device.

24

Last of all, the designer will turn to the half-title. Ideally, this will encapsulate in miniature the typography of the title page (particularly the book title) and of the chapter headings. This page or its verso may have, in addition, to carry such impedimenta as blurbs, series titles and lists of books by the same author or in the same series: these are best dealt with in a carefully planned but plain and discreet style.

We have touched repeatedly on illustration, and it is now time to deal with this important component of many books in some detail. Any illustrations that have to be included in a book will inevitably have a considerable influence: on its format, mode of production (and perhaps mode of composition), layout and general appearance. It is therefore only sensible that the designer should be thoroughly involved in any discussions about the kinds of illustration to be employed and how they are to be reproduced, and in their commissioning.

At its least compelling, as in simple mathematical diagrams and chemical rings, illustrative material can be subordinated to the design of the book. (So of course can a handful of maps or the odd family tree, though equally it is possible, and little more expensive, to make these into an attractive feature of the book: instead of being typeset they may be hand-lettered, and instead of being in the text they may be printed separately, perhaps in two colours, on coloured stock. If there is only one such feature it may be repeated on the front and back endpapers, though these would be lost from a library copy when it was rebound.) All line figures should be drawn in black ink on stiff white Bristol board, tracing paper, Kodatrace or hard white paper. Lettering may be added by the artist, but it is usually best for the publisher to have the lettering set and proofed and then pasted down in position, either on the artwork itself or on an overlay. Such artwork will usually have to be commissioned from a freelance artist or drawing studio, but sometimes the author, particularly if he works in, say, a scientific or geographical department of a university, is in a position to have his illustrations drawn, and as this may represent a considerable saving in cost it is worth the designer's while to brief the author carefully so as to ensure that the result is satisfactory. Copy for the lettering, and instructions for any tint areas to be added by the printer, should be shown either on an overlay or on a Xerox of the line artwork.

More inherently decorative are line and halftone illustrations for children's books and occasional classics such as those published by the Folio Society, and most photographs; the pictures are indeed the substance of children's picture books and at least the prime ingredient in art books. In both these cases, the establishment of page size and the artist's choice of format for his illustrations must be complementary decisions. Typographical design becomes a matter respectively of unobtrusive large-type readability, and of discreet sympathy with both the weight and the historical flavour of the reproductions. The great majority of art books, and virtually all children's picture books, are printed by litho, but letterpress printing on art paper is still used to bring up sharp detail, as, for example, in the reproduction of miniatures and for high-resolution biological photographic enlargements. Gravure printing is employed, both for medium to long runs of high-quality photographic work, and also for very long runs of low-price colour work. Collotype, which is expensive and almost unobtainable, is capable of fine reproduction of such delicate originals as pencil drawings and photographs of coins.

The most usual problem with book illustration concerns the handling, not of two or three or a bookful of illustrations, but of, say, two dozen. In a short-run book, otherwise ideally suited to printing by letterpress from type, the cost of a dozen or more blocks may be enough to tip the balance to the litho process, which of course requires no blocks. This is particularly true if the illustrations be halftones, since halftone blocks are more expensive than line, and require separate printing on art paper and separate handling in the bindery. Litho printing permits illustrations in the text to encroach upon the margins if necessary: this is feasible in letterpress also, but creates a slight extra cost as the furniture (spacing material) around the illustrations has to be specially arranged. The size of an illustration in the text should be judged in relation to its subject, its weight, the measure and page size of the book, and the size of the lettering (if any), which should be smaller than the text type. Most illustrations benefit from some reduction, by perhaps a third or a quarter, as this tends to sharpen up the image and to hide imperfections; and minimising the number of reduction factors helps to maintain consistency of line thickness, and tends to save on reproduction costs.

There is much to be said for instructing the printer that all illustrations in the text (and tables too perhaps) should fall at the head of the page. Placing the illustrations as close as possible to their textual reference can create a haphazard effect. Landscaped illustrations, those which the reader must turn the book sideways to read, should not face portrait (upright) illustrations, and should be placed on left-hand pages, in obedience to a comfortable convention which also prefers profile reproductions to face 'into' the book. In a centred design, illustrations look best centred on the text measure. In asymmetrical work the placing of illustrations in relation to the text area is more critical and should be handled *ad hoc* by the designer.

Here it may be useful to consider the question of bleeding. This is a dangerous device in the hands of a careless designer, who by bleeding a painting may spoil its balance, or by bleeding all the halftones may overpower the text. It can on the other hand be extremely effective, particularly for an enlarged detail and for dramatic photographs. As the printer is likely to ask for a bigger sheet, or to take a larger trim off a standard sheet, bleeding usually entails either a higher paper cost, or a smaller trimmed page.

The design of illustrations printed separately from the text – because by a different process, or on a different paper, or in colour – can be either based closely on the design of the text pages, using the same margins, or based specifically on the content and weight of the illustrations; both approaches have their merits, deriving respectively from consistency and from harmonious contrast. A decision to bleed these illustrations has, of course, no effect on the sheet size of the text paper.

We have alluded repeatedly to paper, which is – or can be – much more than a mere vehicle for the printed image. A sympathetic paper responds to the printing medium, the type and the illustrations to produce that satisfying sensation of inevitability which is the hallmark of good printing. For any job there exists an ideal paper, and a range of compromises. Short of the ideal, which is likely to be expensive, the most sympathetic paper will not necessarily be the dearest. But pressure from publishers anxious to economise has tended both to degrade the quality of paper and to reduce the available range. The designer's dilemma recurs: whether to continue the search for a sympathetic, characterful paper that will encourage and enhance good printing, and face perhaps a battle over its cost, or to settle for something safe, if rather bland.

Limited ranges of standard papers – whether supplied by printer or publisher – are employed for web printing of long-run colour work and pocket-format paperbacks, and on shorter-run mini-web litho presses. A number of book printers carry sheet stocks of standard papers also, for flatbed letterpress and sheet-fed rotary letterpress work. There is often some advantage in using these stock lines, if they seem suitable: the printer is familiar with them, he takes the responsibility for printing well on them, and he will have bought a large supply at a keen price.

Litho printing, where the image lies on the surface of the paper, is not a demanding process, since almost any image can be reasonably printed on almost any paper. Litho can, however, seem rather flat, and there is a lot to be said for using a paper which complements in colour and finish the weight and style of the text and illustration, and has besides some character of its own. For ultimate fidelity to a finely-detailed halftone image, art (glazed) paper, which may be had in glossy or matt finishes, cannot be matched. Art paper, however, is heavy, expensive and not in itself particularly attractive, and for the run of illustrated books a coated cartridge (lightly glazed), of which the market offers a wide variety, or a twin-wire cartridge will carry the screened image almost as well and at less cost.

The process of flatbed letterpress printing is altogether more sensitive to the choice of paper. We have seen how the true form of metal type is revealed only in printing, when it is impressed into the paper and slightly thickened through squash. Many of the hot-metal typefaces in use today, such as Bembo and Garamond, are based very closely on historical models cut at a time when books were printed on soft, absorbent off-white antique wove paper, and modern settings in such faces still look best when printed on paper of that kind. Other hot-metal faces of recent design, such as Times New Roman and Ehrhardt, seem at home on any paper. In the same way, half-tone blocks require a smooth surface, in relation to the fineness of the screen used: coarse, absorbent paper, such as newsprint and antique wove, will accept a screen no finer than 85 lines to the inch; a good MF will print 100 lines; 120 and finer require art paper. For most novels and (more-or-less un-illustrated) non-fiction there exists a wide range of book papers (ranging that is from rubbish to good), available in a range of colours, bulks and finishes. The slightly rough finish that most people would recognise as conventional book paper is known as antique wove; smoother, slightly less bulky MF versions are obtained by repeated rolling under pressure. There are also, of course, antique laids and other more-or-less *de luxe* papers at more-or-less *de luxe* prices.

Various other considerations have to be taken into account in the selection of paper. Two which are to some extent related are bulk and opacity. It is often said that the buying public does not care for a thin book, or for thin paper. The evidence for this is not adduced, and it may or may not be true. But what is quite certain is that excessive bulk in paper is an enemy of quality in printing. It is also inefficient: being bulky, it tends to be fluffy, which necessitates more frequent washing-up on machine, and this costs the publisher more (though its proponents argue that it gives the appearance – the illusion – of better value for money). There should of course be some correlation between bulk, weight and format: what may seem unduly heavy in a small book may seem just right in a large one. The use of thin papers, necessary for extra-long books, raises the alternative problem of show-through. The two-problems seldom meet in any one book, but when they do a lack of opacity is the lesser evil in plain text, a lack of bulk perhaps in illustrated, particularly photographic, books.

One more problem concerned with paper is the important matter of grain. A bound book should lie flat when opened. If it does not, the chances are that the grain runs across the page, whereas it should, of course, run parallel to the sewing of the spine. This is usually a simple matter to arrange in letterpress printing, and indeed in monochrome litho printing as well. In colour litho, however, particularly four-colour halftone work, the printer may encounter problems of register if the grain runs in the short dimension of the sheet rather than along it – so the binder may have to make the best he can of it.

This is the Hobson's choice all too familiar to binders, who are often expected to make up the time lost by publisher, author and printer, to shave pence off their prices, and still to produce beautiful books. The manufacturing processes involved, resembling a fanciful creation of W. Heath Robinson, for many years resisted mechanisation. The machinery has arrived, however, and is capable of turning out good books; that it does not always do so is due in part at least to ignorance about its benefits and limitations and to lack of precision in the writing of binding specifications.

A well-bound book (strictly speaking the only books that are bound are those that are bound by hand, but to insist on calling mass-produced books 'cased' is pedantic) should be exactly folded, secure at the shoulders, easily read right across the measure, flat when closed and ready to lie flat when open. We have seen that if the grain of the paper runs across the page the open book is likely not to lie flat, and another cause of this problem is over-tight sewing.

Adhesive ('perfect' or unsewn) binding, though now well developed, strong and reliable, also can cause the pages of the open book to lift, to the point where an unsewn paperback may always revert to the closed position even with the reader's hand in it. The type line in such a book may well disappear into the back margin, whence it can be retrieved only by the drastic and irrevocable action of breaking down the spine. A book which does not lie flat when closed is said to be warped, and warping boards have troubled the binding trade inexplicably, unpredictably and at vast expense over many years. The use of greyboards rather than strawboards seems to have done something to ameliorate this perennial headache.

Most books that are sewn are now sewn in 32-page sections. By comparison with sewing in 16s this makes for a slightly more stepped effect on the foredge, and a less evenly rounded back (as well as halving the options for the placing of separately-printed plates); but sewing is a substantial cost, and halving the number of sections to be sewn produces a useful saving. Extra-thin paper can be sewn in 48s or 64s. Partly because of the use of thicker sections, partly because of inadequacy in this particular mechanised process, mechanised rounding-and-backing is not nearly as good as the handmade variety: this may explain the growing popularity of the rigid-board flatback style, which can look very neat and should not diminish the book's ability to open well and to lie flat. We have said that adhesive binding can now be strong, secure and attractive; it is also significantly cheaper than sewn binding (despite the loss of about 3 mm due to the cut-off back), and is widely used for cased novels and cheaper non-fiction as well as the great bulk of mass-market paperbacks. A decision to adhesive-bind has certain implications for the design: there may be severe restrictions on the placing of separate plates; illustrations cannot be taken into the back, or bled at the spine trim (because ink inhibits the secure adhesion of the glue); an adhesive-bound book will be narrower than a sewn book printed on the same paper, by the width of the spine trim; and, whether cased or paperback, the spine will be narrower.

Increasing (and improving) mechanisation has brought together several processes (notably printing, folding, gathering, and sewing or adhesive binding). This change – together with daunting rises in hand-labour costs and the general acceptance of litho printing for most illustrated books – has greatly reduced both capacity and demand for benchwork, the tipping-in, wrapping-round, insetting, inserting and special folding of plates (other than those grouped together as complete sections) and fold-out maps.

We come now to the blocking or stamping. This is usually restricted to the spine of the case, though it is often possible – depending on which way the case is fed into the blocking machine, and on the width and number of foil reels employed – to block simultaneously on the front board. A few books, usually high-priced works of reference, are still blocked in real gold, but imitation gold (or silver or aluminium) is now the norm, quite often superimposed on a coloured foil panel. Again, a few books are blocked with hand-cut brasses, but patent copper dies, made and etched photomechanically, are the norm; though occasionally they are reproduced from a hand-lettered original, a typeset original is much more usual. The design of these little dies is surprisingly difficult: problems arise from long words, narrow or uncertain spines, the articulation of title and subtitle, the negative image, as it were, of light type on a dark background, and above all perhaps from the extreme sensitivity of this medium to the slightest error in spacing. A common, and commonly regrettable, device is the use of the spine lettering from the jacket as the image blocked on the binding. It seldom works well – owing perhaps to the slight shock of seeing the 'same' image used in two totally different ways, but more likely to the fact that lettering entirely appropriate to a jacket, combined maybe with a picture and intended to attract customers across the street and into the bookshop, can look merely crude stamped in metallic foil on cloth or cloth substitute.

The selectors of the National Book League's annual exhibition of British book design and production regularly lament drab bindings, a perfectly fair criticism both of lettering design and also of most binding materials. The best cloths, buckrams and art canvases are lively and attractive on their own account, and handling a book bound in them is a visual and tactile pleasure. The vast majority of cased books, however, are bound in cheap cloth or cloth substitutes, the best of which are acceptable but hardly lively, and the worst, rubbish. The more expensive cloth substitutes, such as Linson, are probably more durable than cheap cloth; but, in general, price is here a fair guide to quality. The temptation not infrequently arises, when the costings of a serious work of non-fiction look high, to save on the binding material. Since the purpose of and market for the book remain unchanged, this saving is usually not appropriate.

It is a paradox that the binding, a part of the book which is to last and to survive many re-readings is often produced as cheaply as it possibly can be, using indifferent materials and fairly insensitive production processes, but is ephemerally wrapped in a *de luxe* four-colour art paper jacket on which, commonly, no expense has been spared. This is not the place, however, to argue this point.

The original function of the jacket, now almost lost to sight (except for expensive reference books, never likely to be displayed for sale in a bookshop), was simply to protect the binding. Most jackets and paperback covers are today conceived primarily as posters, advertising the existence and nature of the book they enclose, and it is not unusual for a commercial publisher to employ an art editor especially responsible for commissioning the illustration and design of jackets. But no jacket design need be dull even though it may well, and sensibly, be done under stringent financial limitations. It is easy enough to create an arresting design in the four process colours; it is amazing what can be done with two.

There is often a great temptation to use an illustration on a jacket or cover, and this is on the whole an appropriate temptation to fall for. The jacket's

Jackets and covers   prime function today is to sell the book: not just out of the bookshop, but into it, and indeed into the hearts of the publisher's salesmen. As long as the picture is an attractive one (and it may be a photograph, painting or drawing), and does not mislead either as to the kind of book or as to whether the book itself is illustrated, it may well be used. It will need careful handling if it is not to dominate, or be dominated by, the title and author's name.

Failing an illustration, the treatment may be 'graphic', calligraphic, or typographical. Graphic design employs the resources of ornament, colour and lettering in a very much freer way than is possible with plain type, particularly metal type (though a metal-type design may possess an extra dimension through its impression into the paper).

Calligraphy is flourishing today and several distinguished calligraphers are producing ingenious, elegant designs. One great virtue of handwriting, by pen or brush, is its ability to fit a large number of words into a small space without apparent difficulty.

Usually the back and flaps of a jacket and the cover are put to work to carry blurbs for this and other books. Sometimes, however, it is possible to design an 'all-round' jacket that will encourage generous displays in bookshop windows.

The whole book   The designer must be at all times a mediator, an interpreter: through his imagination, his experience and his knowledge of the art, craft and science of printing he converts the typescript into a book and expresses the author's words clearly and sympathetically to the reader. And yet his design for a clear text, however good in itself, is not enough; his integration into the text of the illustrations, their printing on pleasing paper, the book's insertion into a strong binding within an irresistible jacket, are needed to fuse the whole book into the harmony that seems easy and irresistible.